# 10 MINDSETS TO EMBRACE

For Teenage Success, Happiness,
and A Determined Path in Life

## CHARLES E TYLER

# FOREWARD

Welcome to "*10 Mindsets To Embrace: For Teenage Success, Happiness, and a Determined Path In Life!.*" Get ready to dive into a pool of wisdom, insights, and practical guidance that will shape the course of your life.

As the author of this book, I've had the privilege of accumulating years of experience and knowledge. While my teenage years might seem like a distant memory, the challenges and triumphs of that period remain etched in my mind. That's why I've poured my heart and soul into crafting these mindsets— sage advice designed to help you navigate the unique journey of adolescence.

I made this book short but sweet so that I can go straight to the point in each chapter while providing valuable insight into each mindset discussed. I am proud to present my first book, inspired by countless stories of perseverance, determination, and growth. Though many great books teach similar lessons, I wanted to write my own book focused on the mindsets I believe are most important. I also added my own unique perspective to the chapters to provide a fresh take on these mindsets and help you better understand them.

Now, let's talk about these mindsets. Imagine them as the keys to unlock the doors of possibility. Each is like a secret code guiding you through challenges and propelling you toward greatness. And yes, I promise, there are no secret handshakes required.

As you flip through these pages, you'll discover stories, quotes, practical exercises, and even a few teen perspectives that'll make you say, "Hey, that's totally me!" Whether you're dealing with algebra anxiety or friendship fiascos, these mindsets have your back. Think of them as your trusty sidekicks in the grand adventure of growing up.

So, whether you're reading this in your room, during a study break, or even sneakily under your desk during class (hey, I won't tell), remember you're not alone on this journey. Let's learn, learn, learn, and leap into the world of mindsets together. Because who knows, maybe one day you'll be the one writing a book and sharing your own tales of teenage wisdom.

Wishing you a journey filled with growth and greatness,

Mr. Tyler

# CONTENTS

# INTRODUCTION

> "The future belongs to those who believe in the beauty of their dreams."
>
> **- Eleanor Roosevelt**

Welcome to an extraordinary journey that awaits you! Envision a world where your dreams materialize into reality and joy accompanies you every step of the way. Exciting, isn't it? Well, fasten your seatbelt, for we are about to embark on a life-changing adventure together!

Within the pages of this book lies a treasure trove of ten powerful mindsets, each capable of empowering you to navigate through the challenges of adolescence and pave the path to a successful and fulfilling life. These mindsets are the keys to unlocking your boundless potential, thus transforming your dreams into reality as you embark on a determined path toward greatness.

Are you ready to embrace challenges, conquer setbacks, and foster strong relationships? Do you eagerly desire to cultivate a positive self-image, practice empathy, and master the art of time management? If so, this book is your trusted guide. Through inspiring stories, reflections from your teenage perspective, practical exercises, and valuable insights, you will discover the transformative power of these mindsets.

Let's dive into Part One and explore the first five mindsets that lay the foundation for your success and happiness. You'll learn how to embrace the growth mindset by seeing challenges as opportunities for growth and believing in your capacity to learn and improve. Additionally, we'll delve into the power of constructive criticism, learning from it to grow and improve while being open to feedback from others for personal development. Cultivating gratitude and empathy will also be explored, showing you how to appreciate the good things in life and extend compassion and understanding to others. Lastly, you'll discover the significance of unwavering determination, setting ambitious goals, and pursuing your dreams with relentless focus. These essential traits will strengthen your core, thus enabling you to confront any obstacle that crosses your path.

In Part Two, we'll uncover the remaining five mindsets, propelling you even further on your journey to greatness. You'll learn the art of proactivity and initiative, taking charge in all aspects of life and creating opportunities for yourself rather than waiting for them to come. Embracing a positive self-image will be paramount, nurturing self-worth and self-confidence while embracing your uniqueness and talents.

Furthermore, you'll come to appreciate the importance of respecting others and embracing diversity, treating everyone with kindness, and fostering a harmonious and inclusive environment. Staying curious and open-minded will be another vital mindset, encouraging you to embrace new experiences and embody curiosity and adaptability.

Last but not least, we'll delve into the crown jewel — cultivating emotional intelligence. Developing your self-awareness and emotional intelligence will empower you to understand and effectively manage your emotions, thereby propelling you toward unparalleled success.

As a special bonus, you'll find powerful quotes with explanations from famous individuals at the end of each chapter before the conclusion. These quotes will serve as an extra dose of inspiration, showcasing how remarkable individuals have lived by the very mindsets we are exploring together. From the wisdom of Steve Jobs to insights from other extraordinary figures, these quotes will uplift and motivate you on your journey.

So, let's make this adventure unforgettable as we unlock the secrets to success and happiness. Fasten your seatbelt, open your mind and heart, and let's begin this extraordinary journey of embracing mindsets that will shape your destiny and make you shine like the star you truly are!

# Part 1
# Laying the Foundation

---

# EMBRACE THE GROWTH MINDSET

✓ Embracing Challenges as Opportunities for Growth
✓ Believing in Your Ability to Learn and Improve

Hey there! Welcome to the first chapter of our awesome journey! This chapter is all about the super cool *Growth Mindset*—the key to turning challenges into opportunities for growth and becoming even more amazing at whatever you set your mind to. You're going to love this mindset—it's like having a secret power that makes you unstoppable! Let's dive in and discover how to embrace it and become the best version of yourself.

## Embracing Challenges as Opportunities for Growth

Life can be tough sometimes, right? But guess what? With the Growth Mindset, you'll recognize challenges as exciting opportunities to become even better! Instead of feeling scared or giving up, you'll be like, "Bring it on!" Every time you face a challenge, you'll know that it's an opportunity to learn and grow, just like leveling up in a game! So don't be afraid to take risks and face those challenges head-on cause you're going to come out even stronger and wiser!

## | Inspiring Story

Let me introduce you to Sarah, an incredible artist who dreams of showcasing her artwork in a fancy gallery. At first, she was hesitant and afraid of facing rejection. Doubts crept into her mind, making her wonder if she was good enough to make it happen. But then, something amazing happened: Sarah embraced the Growth Mindset. She decided to take a chance and give it her all. Even when some galleries turned her down, she didn't let it bring her down. Instead, she saw those rejections as opportunities to learn and grow.

Sarah used the feedback she received to improve her art, refine her techniques, and experiment with new styles. With each rejection, she became even more determined to prove herself and showcase her artistic talent. And guess what? All that hard work and determination paid off! One awesome gallery saw the potential in her art and loved what they saw. They offered Sarah the opportunity to showcase her artwork, and she felt like she had become a superhero!

Sarah's growth mindset not only made her art better, but it also made her feel unstoppable. She realized that it's not about being perfect from the start but about embracing challenges and growing from them. Every setback became a stepping stone toward success. So, the next time you have a dream or face a challenge, remember Sarah's story. Embrace the Growth Mindset, and don't be afraid to take risks and learn from your failures. Like Sarah, you have the power to turn setbacks into opportunities and transform into a superhero of your own journey! Keep believing in yourself, keep growing, and keep chasing those dreams! You've got this!

## | Practical Exercise

One exercise that can help you apply the concept of a Growth Mindset to overcome the fear of failure and gain confidence is by challenging yourself to step out of your comfort zone and pursue something you've been holding back due to fear. Hey, what's the worst that could happen? Probably just mild embarrassment and a few funny stories to tell your friends!

To begin, take a moment to think about something you really want to do but have been hesitant to try because of the fear of failure. It could be learning a new skill, starting a new business venture, or even pursuing a personal goal. Please write it down in a clear and specific manner. Now, imagine how adopting a Growth Mindset can transform your approach to this particular endeavor. Embrace the belief that your abilities and talents can be developed through dedication, effort, and learning from mistakes. Instead of viewing the potential outcome as a measure of your worth or ability, see it as an opportunity for growth and personal development.

Consider how seeing this experience as an opportunity for growth can make you feel more confident to give it a try. Recognize that even if you encounter setbacks or face challenges, these valuable learning opportunities will contribute to your personal growth and development. By approaching the situation with a Growth Mindset, you can cultivate resilience, persistence, and a willingness to learn from your experiences. As you embrace the idea of growth and recognize challenges as opportunities for learning and development, you will likely find yourself feeling more confident to take that initial step toward your desired goal. The fear of failure will gradually diminish as you start to see failure not as a reflection of your abilities but as a stepping stone in your journey towards progress and success.

Remember, the key is to maintain a growth-oriented perspective throughout the process. Embrace challenges, learn from setbacks, and celebrate your progress along the way. By adopting a Growth Mindset, you can transform your fear of failure into a catalyst for personal growth, ultimately leading you to an increased confidence and a willingness to take on new challenges.

So, take a leap of faith, embrace the growth mindset, and give that long-held aspiration a try. You never know what you can achieve until you take that first step toward growth and development.

## Believing in Your Ability to Learn and Improve

Okay, here's the secret sauce of the Growth Mindset—believing in yourself! You know that thing you think you're not good at? Well, with the Growth Mindset, you'll know that you can totally get better at it! You've got the power to learn and improve like a pro! It's like having a magic wand that helps you get smarter and more skilled over time. So, believe in yourself because you're capable of awesome things!

## Valuable Insight

Here's the inside scoop: Every time you try something new or face a challenge, you're growing and learning, even if it feels tough. So, don't get discouraged if you make mistakes or things don't work out right away. Keep moving forward, and remember, you're getting better every step of the way!

## Inspiring Story

Meet Michael, a remarkable high school student who, at one point, believed he lacked proficiency in chemistry. However, a profound transformation occurred when he wholeheartedly embraced the Growth Mindset, opening the door to a world of endless possibilities. With a newfound sense of determination, Michael confidently declared, "Hey, I can totally improve!" Encouraged by this mindset, he sought help from his teachers and friends, recognizing that learning is a collaborative journey.

Undeterred by initial challenges, Michael wholeheartedly devoted himself to practice, demonstrating the tenacity of a true champion. As the days turned into weeks and the weeks turned into months, Michael witnessed an astonishing improvement in his analytical skills. Concepts that once seemed daunting now appeared conquerable, and his confidence also soared. Michael's growth mindset helped him ace chemistry and transformed him into a self-proclaimed scientific genius. His success in chemistry became a stepping stone for other aspects of his life. Michael realized that by embracing the Growth Mindset, he could overcome any obstacle that came his way. He began approaching every challenge with an unwavering belief in his capacity to learn and grow. This newfound perspective instilled within him a passion for continuous self-improvement, empowering him to excel not only in academics but in various areas of his life.

Michael's journey serves as a testament to the incredible power of adopting a Growth Mindset. It unlocked his academic potential and ignited a lifelong love for learning and self-discovery. With the belief that effort and perseverance can lead to greatness, Michael's future knows no bounds. He stands as a living example of how a growth mindset can pave the way for limitless opportunities and personal growth, inspiring those around him to embrace the same transformative outlook on life.

## | Inspiring Quote for Chapter 1

"The only way to do great work is to love what you do." - Steve Jobs (Co-founder and former CEO of Apple)

**What does this quote have to do with this chapter? Here is what this means:**

- The quote emphasizes that to excel in your work and impress others, you must genuinely love what you do; it cannot be faked or forced.

- This connection relates to a growth mindset, which revolves around the belief that improvement comes through practice and effort.
- With a growth mindset, you become eager to invest time and effort into improving yourself because you find it enjoyable and rewarding.
- Having a passion for something motivates you to seek challenges, embrace learning, take risks, and seek constructive feedback to enhance your skills.
- To achieve remarkable mastery in a particular field, such as reaching a go-pro level, discover what excites you about learning, hard work, and skill development.
- When you love what you do, it won't feel like work, and you'll be enthusiastic about your growth journey.

Special note from the author: The key is to let your curiosity guide you to the work you love. This passion and drive should enable you to achieve greatness.

## | Conclusion

Great job finishing the first chapter of our journey! You're now a Growth Mindset pro! Remember, challenges are just like mini-adventures that help you level up in life. Believe in yourself and know that you can learn and improve like a pro! In the next chapter, we'll dive into the awesome power of embracing criticism and how it can make you even stronger and cooler. Keep rockin' it, and I'll see you there!

Embracing criticism is a fundamental aspect of developing a Growth Mindset. Instead of fearing feedback or viewing it as a personal attack, we'll learn to see it as an opportunity for growth and self-improvement. It's a chance to gain valuable insights and identify areas where we can enhance our skills and abilities.

Remember, criticism doesn't define your worth or potential. It's merely a stepping stone on your journey to becoming the best version of yourself. So, stay open-minded, stay curious, and keep pushing yourself to reach new heights!

Get ready for the next chapter, where we'll discover the secrets of handling criticism like a true champion. Until then, keep your mindset positive, your spirit adventurous, and your determination unwavering. You've got this! See you soon!

## CHAPTER 2

# EMBRACE THE POWER OF CONSTRUCTIVE CRITICISM

✓ Being Open to Feedback for Personal Development

Welcome to Chapter 2, where we'll explore the transformative power of **constructive criticism**—a valuable tool that can propel us toward growth and self-improvement.

*Constructive criticism* is not designed to tear us down; instead, it offers valuable insights that help us become the best version of ourselves. By being open to feedback from others, including parents, family members, loved ones, and teachers, we can use it as a stepping stone towards our success. Let's learn how to embrace constructive criticism with an open mind and a growth-oriented perspective.

## | Being Open to Feedback for Personal Development

In this mindset, we understand that being open to feedback is crucial to personal development. When we are receptive to feedback from our loved ones and teachers, we gain valuable perspectives that may have been otherwise overlooked. Being open to feedback shows our willingness to learn and grow. Let's be champions of humility and approach feedback with gratitude, recognizing its potential to elevate us to new heights.

## | Inspiring Story

Meet Jake, an exceptionally gifted artist passionate about sharing his creations with the world. When Jake encountered constructive criticism from his family and teachers, he faced a pivotal moment that could have discouraged him from pursuing his artistic dreams. However, Jake possessed a unique perspective and an unwavering commitment to growth.

Rather than letting criticism dampen his spirits, Jake embraced it as a valuable tool for improvement. He understood that constructive feedback was not a reflection of his inadequacy but an opportunity to refine and elevate his artistic style. With the growth mindset guiding him, Jake eagerly absorbed every piece of advice, using it to hone his skills and expand his creative horizons.

As time passed, Jake's artwork blossomed into a stunning tapestry of expression and ingenuity. His commitment to improvement and his ability to welcome criticism as a stepping stone toward excellence became the bedrock of his success. People around him began to notice the transformation, and Jake became a true inspiration for his artistic prowess and courage in accepting and embracing feedback.

Jake's journey holds a powerful lesson for all of us. It reminds us that embracing constructive criticism from our loved ones and mentors can be the catalyst for unlocking our full potential. It is not a sign of weakness but a testament to our resilience and willingness to grow. Just as Jake's art flourished when he embraced feedback, so can our own endeavors thrive when we approach criticism with an open heart and a growth-oriented mindset.

Jake's story serves as a reminder that when met with determination and a desire to improve, criticism can be a powerful force for transformation and progress. It encourages us to recognize constructive feedback not as a hurdle but as a gift that empowers us to reach new heights and become the best version of ourselves. Through Jake's example, we are inspired to cultivate the courage to seek feedback, cherish the growth it brings, and embark on a journey of continuous improvement and personal growth.

## | Practical Exercise

Think back to a recent school project or extracurricular activity where you received feedback from your parents, family, or teachers. Take some time to reflect on their specific advice and consider how you can use it to improve your work.

Approach this as an opportunity for growth. Feedback allows us to identify areas where we can develop our skills. With an open and positive mindset, you can turn constructive criticism into fuel for continuous improvement.

To put the advice into action:

Choose a recent project where you received feedback. Think of a paper, assignment, or activity that your parents, family, or teachers critiqued.

Review the feedback in detail. Note any specifics on content, structure, presentation, or other aspects. Hone in on the key ways they felt you could improve.

Pinpoint areas for improvement. Based on the feedback, what skills could benefit from more focus? Is it research, writing, or time management? Identify your weak spots.

Brainstorm practical solutions. How can you directly address those weak spots? By researching more or mentorship? Targeted practice? New techniques? Get creative with strategies.

Make an action plan. Break solutions into manageable tasks with realistic timelines. Seek support from teachers, parents, and mentors too.

By thoughtfully implementing feedback, you can see real growth with each project. The path of improvement is gradual, but each step forward builds your skills. Keep an open mind, stay positive, and use criticism to fuel your development.

## | Inspiring Quote for Chapter 2:

"Criticism is something you can easily avoid by saying nothing, doing nothing, and being nothing." – Aristotle (An ancient Greek philosopher)

**What does this quote have to do with this chapter? Here is what this means:**

- Criticism can hurt your feelings, but it's part of growing up.
- Criticism happens, especially when you put yourself out there because you are making things happen.
- You can avoid criticism by doing/being nothing. But doing nothing and being nothing stops your growth and purpose.
- Keep sharing, learning, and being yourself. That's more important than avoiding criticism.
- Believe in yourself and keep moving forward, even if you're criticized.
- It's a sign that you are taking action (doing something with your life) and striving for greatness.
- Embrace feedback, and let it guide you on your path to becoming the best version of yourself.

Special note from the author: This quote indicates that criticism has a silencing effect, but we must find the courage to pursue our truths despite potential disapproval. Progress and fulfillment require withstanding criticism.

## | Conclusion

Congratulations on embracing the mindset of being open to feedback and using constructive criticism as a tool for personal development! By remaining open-minded, you show a willingness to learn and grow, and that's a powerful trait. Remember that feedback from your loved ones and teachers is not meant to bring you down; it's intended to elevate you and help you reach new heights. Keep cultivating this mindset, and you'll discover the immense power of self-improvement on your journey to success.

## CHAPTER 3

# GRATITUDE AND EMPATHY

- ✓ Cultivating Gratitude and Spreading Positivity Everywhere
- ✓ Cultivating Empathy

Welcome to Chapter 3, where we'll explore two incredible qualities—***gratitude and empathy***! Imagine having the power to spread joy and kindness everywhere you go. Well, that's exactly what gratitude and empathy do! These amazing traits make the world a better place, and they're right within us. Did you know that? Let's learn how to cultivate these remarkable qualities and become champions of kindness and understanding!

## Cultivating Gratitude and Spreading Positivity Everywhere

Gratitude is like a magical force that brightens everyone's day. It's about appreciating the little things and being thankful for what we have. When we practice gratitude, we become champions of positivity! Gratitude boosts our happiness and makes us feel amazing. Let's spread this extraordinary magic and make the world shine with thankfulness!

## | Inspiring Story

Meet Maya, a remarkable teenager who decided to embark on a beautiful journey of gratitude. She discovered the power of a simple yet profound practice of keeping a gratitude journal. Every day, without fail, Maya dedicated a few moments to jotting down three things she was thankful for. It could be the vibrant views of a breathtaking sunset that painted the sky, the warmth of a friend's kindness that touched her heart, or the delicious flavors of a family dinner that delighted her taste buds. With each entry, Maya's heart filled with appreciation and joy.

As she continued this daily ritual of gratitude, Maya noticed an incredible transformation unfolding within herself. The more she immersed herself in the spirit of thankfulness, the more her happiness seemed to radiate from within. A newfound sense of contentment and positivity embraced her, and she began to exude an aura of genuine joy that was contagious to those around her.

Maya's friends and family couldn't help but notice the change in her demeanor. They were inspired by the radiant glow of happiness she displayed, and they were curious to learn about the secret behind her transformation. Maya gladly shared her gratitude journal practice with them, encouraging them to give it a try. It wasn't long before her loved ones also began to discover the magic of gratitude.

The ripple effect of Maya's gratitude journey was far-reaching. Her own life brightened with newfound appreciation and fulfillment, and she became a beacon of light for others. Maya's simple act of counting her blessings and expressing thankfulness resonated deeply with everyone she touched. Her attitude of gratitude changed lives and ignited a flame of hope and positivity in the hearts of those around her.

Maya's story serves as a heartwarming reminder of the immense power of gratitude. Through her daily practice of thankfulness, she not only cultivated a sense of well-being and happiness within herself, but she also became an inspiration for others to find beauty and joy in the small moments of life. With a heart filled with gratitude, Maya continues to touch lives, reminding us of all the abundant blessings that surround us and the transformative power of appreciating the wonders that life offers us each day.

## Practical Exercise:

Start your gratitude journal today! Write down three things you are thankful for every day for a week.

Here's how:

1. Get a notebook or notes app to write in.
2. Spend a few minutes each day writing down three things you're grateful for.

3. They could be small or big, like friends, food, or nature. Anything that brought you joy.
4. Keep it up the whole week! Consistency matters.
5. At the end of the week, reflect on how you feel. More positive?
6. Share some entries or talk about them with family/friends.
7. Think about keeping the journal moving forward. Gratitude takes practice but improves your well-being!
8. Write down your gifts, big and small. Recognize the good things around you.
9. Let gratitude brighten your days and outlook!

In conclusion, starting a gratitude journal is a simple yet powerful practice that can bring more positivity and joy into your life. You can cultivate a mindset of appreciation by taking just a few minutes each day to write down three things you're thankful for. Acknowledging these gifts can improve your overall well-being, whether it's the small everyday pleasures or the big moments of happiness. Remember to stay consistent throughout the week; at the end of it, take a moment to reflect on how you feel. Sharing your entries with loved ones can also foster connection and positivity. So, let gratitude be your guiding light, brightening your days and outlook on life.

## Cultivating Empathy

*The Power of Understanding:* Empathy is like having a special ability to understand others' feelings. When we cultivate empathy, we become champions of compassion! We listen with an open heart, walk in someone else's shoes, and show kindness and support. Let's be champions who lift others up and make them feel seen and cared for!

## | Valuable Insight

By expanding on the importance of empathy, we discover that it is a powerful tool that enables us to forge meaningful and lasting connections with others. When we actively seek to understand someone's feelings, experiences, and perspectives, we not only deepen our relationships, but we also become better friends, siblings, and members of our community.

Empathy allows us to put ourselves in others' shoes, to see the world through their eyes, and to feel what they feel. This profound understanding creates a strong bond of trust and support, as people recognize that they can confide in us without fear of judgment or criticism.

In our roles as friends, empathy enables us to be there for our companions during both joyous and challenging times. It allows us to celebrate their victories with genuine happiness and to offer a comforting shoulder during moments of distress. With empathy, we can provide the emotional support and encouragement that fosters a sense of belonging and camaraderie.

Within our families, empathy also plays a crucial role in fostering harmony and cohesion. By understanding the emotions and needs of our siblings and family members, we cultivate an environment of open communication and mutual respect.

Empathy allows us to navigate through conflicts with understanding, seeking resolution through empathy-driven conversations rather than resorting to hostility or resentment.

In the broader community, empathy is the foundation for building a compassionate and inclusive society. When we take the time to understand the struggles and experiences of others, we become advocates for positive change. Empathy empowers us to stand alongside those who face adversity, lending our support and working together towards solutions that benefit everyone.

## Inspiring Quote for Chapter 3

As the wise author once said, "Too often, we underestimate the power of a touch, a smile, a kind word, a listening ear, an honest compliment, or the smallest act of caring, all of which have the potential to turn a life around." - Leo Buscaglia (A motivational speaker and writer)

**What does this quote have to do with this chapter? Here is what this means:**

- This quote tells us that sometimes, we don't realize how much of a positive impact simple acts of kindness can have on someone's life.
- It means that even small things like a gentle touch, a friendly smile, a kind word, being a good listener, giving an honest compliment, or showing that you care in a little way can make a big difference in someone's life.

- These small acts of kindness have the power to completely change someone's day or even turn their life around for the better.
- It reminds us that we should never underestimate the power of our actions, no matter how small they may seem, because they can have a huge and positive impact on others.
- So, it's important to be mindful of how we treat others and to always try to be kind and caring, as even the smallest acts of kindness can mean a lot to someone and make a big difference in their life.

Special note from the author: In summary, the quote emphasizes that even the smallest words and acts of caring should not be underestimated for their power to uplift others and forge human bonds. We can all make a difference through simple compassion. I had to learn this, and it changed my life.

## Conclusion

Congratulations on embracing gratitude and empathy—the amazing traits of kindness and understanding! As we journey forward, let's spread gratitude like a magical force and cultivate empathy like a special power. Together, we can make the world a brighter and kinder place! In the next chapter, we'll explore the remarkable power of determination. Get ready to unleash your champion willpower! Keep shining with gratitude and empathy, and I'll see you in the next chapter!

## CHAPTER 4

# THE POWER OF DETERMINATION AND COMMITMENT

✓ Setting Ambitious Goals
✓ Staying Committed and Focused

Welcome to Chapter 4, where we'll delve into the *invincible power of determination,* which is a force that can move mountains and make dreams come true. As teenagers, you have a boundless energy source and a world of opportunities ahead. In this chapter, we'll explore the art of determination and how it empowers you to pursue your dreams with unwavering focus, just like someone trying to learn a hard math problem or excel in a sport.

## Setting Ambitious Goals

In this mindset, we will learn to dream big and set ambitious goals for ourselves. Let's consider a challenging math problem. Imagine you encounter a complex equation that seems like an unsolvable puzzle. Instead of shying or running away, embrace the power of determination. Set the ambitious goal of mastering the problem and solving it with precision. Ambitious goals challenge us to reach beyond our comfort zones and unlock our hidden potential. Let's be champions of courage, always willing to dream big and make our aspirations soar like shooting stars.

## | Inspiring Story:

Ethan, a high school football player, really wanted to improve his game. He was especially nervous about playing in title games because he didn't think he was good enough. This fear was holding him back, but Ethan was determined to overcome it.

He decided to ask his coach for help. His coach was great and gave him all kinds of support. He showed Ethan specific exercises to get better at passing and tackling. But the coach also helped Ethan in other ways. He talked to him about being confident and staying calm during games. They practiced imagining successful plays and keeping a positive attitude.

Ethan's commitment to getting better was strong. He showed up for practice every day, ready to work hard. This determination, along with his coach's guidance, really paid off. He improved a lot in football, but he also became more confident in himself. When Ethan played in a big game without feeling scared, it was a huge victory for him.

Ethan's story is a reminder that if we're committed and determined, we can get better at things that are hard for us. It tells us that it's okay to ask for help and that we can face our fears and succeed with dedication and the right support.

## | Practical Exercise

In the journey of personal growth, determination and commitment play pivotal roles in achieving success. By setting ambitious goals and embracing the mindset of daring to dream big, you, as teenagers and adolescents, can cultivate these essential qualities. This practical exercise aims to help individuals harness their determination and commitment by selecting a challenging subject or skill and setting an ambitious goal for themselves. Whether it's conquering a difficult math problem, mastering a musical instrument, or excelling in a sport, this exercise will demonstrate how determination fuels progress.

### Step 1: Identify a Challenging Subject or Skill

The first step in this practical exercise is to identify a situation that you find challenging. It could be an academic subject, a musical instrument, a sport, or any other area that piques your interest. Selecting a challenging area ensures that you will be motivated to put in the necessary effort and dedication.

### Step 2: Set an Ambitious Goal

Once you have identified the challenging subject or skill, it's time to set an ambitious goal for yourself. This goal should be specific, measurable, attainable, relevant, and time-bound (SMART). For example, if you have selected mastering a musical instrument as a challenge, your goal could be to perform a complex piece flawlessly in front of an audience within six months. Setting an ambitious goal pushes you out of your comfort zone and encourages you to strive for excellence.

## Step 3: Embrace the Mindset of Daring to Dream Big

With your ambitious goal in mind, it is crucial to embrace the mindset of daring to dream big. Believe in your ability to achieve greatness and visualize yourself successfully overcoming challenges. Embracing this mindset will strengthen your determination and commitment, as it helps you stay focused and motivated throughout your journey.

## Step 4: Fuel Your Progress with Determination

Determination is the key to turning your ambitious goal into a reality. It is the unwavering resolve to persist in the face of obstacles and setbacks. Cultivate determination by breaking down your goal into smaller and manageable tasks. Create a plan and commit to following it diligently. Whenever you encounter difficulties, remind yourself of the progress you have made so far and stay focused on the ultimate goal.

## Step 5: Track Your Progress and Celebrate Milestones

As you work towards your ambitious goal, it is essential to track your progress and celebrate milestones along the way. Please keep a record of your achievements, no matter how small they may seem. This will serve as a reminder of your determination and commitment, thus motivating you to keep pushing forward.

## | Staying Committed and Focused

We should understand that determination is not just about setting goals but about staying **committed and focused** on the path to achieving those goals. When you face a complex math problem, you might encounter multiple roadblocks and moments of confusion. However, the power of determination keeps you committed to understanding each step of the solution. Even when the going gets tough, you should refuse to give up. By staying focused and persistent, you build resilience and fortitude in the face of challenges.

## | Teenager's Perspective

As you face this new complex trigonometry problem, you can't help but feel a mixture of excitement and trepidation or fear. It's an intellectual challenge that goes beyond what you've encountered before. But you're not one to back down from a challenge. With a deep breath and a firm resolve, you must decide to embrace the power of determination once again.

You know that this problem won't be solved in a single stroke of brilliance. It will require time, effort, grit, and a lot of perseverance. But you are committed to mastering it. You should remind yourself that, just like the last time, breaking it down into smaller parts is the key to conquering it.

You should seek guidance from your math teacher and engage in discussions with your peers, exchanging ideas and insights. Together, you tackle the problem from different angles, pushing each other to think critically and creatively.

Some days, the complexity of the equation might make you feel overwhelmed. Doubts may creep in, but you must push them aside. You must remind yourself of your determination to succeed. With every setback, you should refuse to give up. Instead, recognize each challenge as an opportunity to learn and grow.

You should practice consistently, working through the problem step by step, even if it means starting from scratch multiple times. The hours will pass, but your focus must be unwavering. And then, suddenly, a moment of clarity emerges. A breakthrough!

The feeling of accomplishment that washes over you is immeasurable. It's not just about solving the math problem; it's about proving to yourself that determination and perseverance can lead to remarkable achievements. The satisfaction you feel is not just in mastering the equation; it's in knowing that you pushed your limits and your determination prevailed.

This experience teaches you a valuable lesson about the power of determination. It shows you that when faced with challenges, staying committed to your goals and pushing through the obstacles can lead to incredible outcomes. You, therefore, carry this lesson with you, knowing that no matter how difficult the path may seem, your determination will guide you toward success in whatever endeavors you pursue.

## | Valuable Insight

Indeed, determination is a journey that extends far beyond achieving immediate success. It's a mindset that propels you forward, guiding you through the twists and turns of life's challenges. As you embark on the path to conquer a difficult math problem or any obstacle in your way, you come to realize that the process itself is just as significant as the end result.

Throughout this journey, setbacks and hurdles may appear, but you should embrace them as opportunities to learn and grow. Doing this turns each setback into a stepping stone, teaching you valuable lessons and revealing areas where improvement is needed. You adapt and refine your approach, gaining a deeper understanding of the problem at hand.

Even the smallest steps you take are significant. With each attempt, you get closer to finding the solution. You should understand that progress might not always be rapid, but every forward movement, no matter how incremental, brings you closer to your goal.

The process of staying committed and focused requires resilience. You must push forward even when the going gets tough, knowing that your determination will see you through the darkest moments. As you face challenges head-on, you must cultivate a strength that runs deeper than any fleeting success.

Beyond mastering math problems, this mindset permeates all aspects of your life. You develop a keen sense of problem-solving that transcends academics. Challenges in other areas become opportunities to apply the same determination and adaptability.

As you persist, you begin to see the transformation within yourself. Your problem-solving skills become sharper, and your capacity to face challenges grows. You become more confident in your abilities, knowing that you can overcome obstacles with dedication and perseverance.

Determination becomes a cornerstone of your character, guiding you through life's ups and downs. You learn that success is not merely reaching the finish line but embracing the journey of growth, resilience, and self-discovery.

## | Inspiring Quote for Chapter 4

A great scientist once said, "*It's not that I'm so smart, it's just that I stay with problems longer.*" – Albert Einstein
(A renowned physicist and Nobel Laureate)

**What does this quote have to do with this chapter? Here is what this means:**

- Einstein was one of the smartest scientists ever, but he said his success wasn't just about intelligence.
- What mattered more was not giving up but persevering through challenging problems until he solved them.
- This takes determination – deciding that you will keep working hard on something without quitting.
- It also takes commitment – promising yourself that you'll keep at the problem no matter how long it takes.
- Smart people fail when they lack determination and commitment. They give up too soon.

- Without pushing through challenges, you'll never achieve great things in school, sports, arts, etc.
- Staying power matters more than just being smart. Using your grit to tackle problems head-on is key.
- Be stubborn, and don't walk away when things get hard. See it through to the end.
- Keep trying different approaches until you find one that works. Don't let setbacks stop you.
- Intelligence on its own is not enough. You need the drive and self-discipline to persist.
- If you commit to staying with tough problems, you can unlock achievements you never thought possible.

Special note from the author: Einstein acknowledged that his ability to persist through obstacles and wrestle for solutions set him apart just as much, if not more, than his outstanding intellect.

## | Conclusion

Congratulations on exploring the power of determination, the force that propels you toward solving complex problems and achieving your dreams. By setting ambitious goals and staying committed with unwavering focus, you hold the key to unlocking your true potential. Your teenage years are a canvas of endless possibilities. I encourage you to embrace the mindset of determination and apply it to conquer every challenge that comes your way. In the next chapter, we'll examine the art of time management and how it empowers you to achieve a healthy balance in life. Keep your eyes on the stars, and I'll see you in the next chapter!

# MASTERING TIME MANAGEMENT

✓ Prioritizing Tasks and Responsibilities
✓ Achieving a Healthy School or Work-Life Balance

## Chapter 5: Mastering Time Management

Welcome to Chapter 5—the final chapter in Part One of this book. Here, we'll explore the secrets of ***mastering time management***—a skill that can make your life easier and more balanced. As teenagers, you have so much on your plate—school, activities, friends, and family. Learning to manage your time wisely will help you achieve your goals and still have time for the things you love. Let's dive in and discover the art of time management!

## Prioritizing Tasks and Responsibilities

Imagine you have a bunch of tasks to complete—homework, chores, and extracurricular activities. To manage your time well, start by making ***a to-do list.*** Write down all the things you need to do and **rank them in order of importance**. Focus on the most crucial tasks first, and you'll feel accomplished as you check them off one by one!

## | Inspiring Story

Meet Sarah, a dynamic and busy teenager who effortlessly juggles her school, sports, and social life. In the past, Sarah used to feel overwhelmed trying to fit everything into her schedule. However, she has since discovered the power of effective time management, transforming her life for the better.

Each morning, Sarah starts her day by creating a comprehensive list of tasks and carefully ranking them by their level of importance. Understanding the significance of her academic responsibilities, she prioritizes schoolwork and other obligations. This means she finishes assignments before engaging in social activities with her friends. While Sarah loves spending time with her friends, she recognizes the value of excelling academically for her future college endeavors. By placing school first, Sarah can enjoy her leisure time guilt-free, knowing she has fulfilled her academic responsibilities.

Despite her desire to socialize constantly, Sarah understands the importance of balance. On days when she has significant tests approaching, she may have to make the tough decision of skipping parties or movies to focus on studying. In these moments, she reminds herself that this temporary sacrifice is vital for her long-term success.

In addition to her academic and social commitments, Sarah is mindful of self-care. She carves out time for activities like reading, exercising, and sharing family dinners. Sarah recognizes that burning out would hinder her overall well-being and productivity. Through strategic planning and careful allocation of time, she achieves a harmonious balance in her packed schedule. Sarah's dedication and effective time management skills allow her to achieve straight A's in school while actively pursuing the activities she loves.

Feeling proud of her responsible time management practices, Sarah has learned the valuable lesson of working hard and playing hard. The key to her success lies in her ability to prioritize wisely and concentrate on what truly matters. As a result, Sarah avoids the overwhelming feeling that often plagues the lives of busy teenagers and instead relishes a fulfilling and satisfying life balance.

## | Practical Exercise

One practical exercise that you can do with time management is creating a to-do list. This document will guide you on how to create an organized and prioritized to-do list for the day or week.

### Step 1: Gather Your Tasks

Before creating your to-do list, take a moment to identify all the tasks that need to be completed. These tasks can include homework assignments, studying for exams, household chores, attending after-school activities, or any other commitments that require your attention.

## Step 2: Write it Down

Once you have a clear idea of all the tasks at hand, write them down on a piece of paper or use a digital to-do list app. This will help you visualize your responsibilities and prevent anything from slipping through the cracks.

## Step 3: Prioritize Your Tasks

After listing all your tasks, it's time to prioritize them. Assess the importance and urgency of each task and assign a priority level to each one. You can use numbers or color coding to indicate the priority. Focusing on the most important tasks first ensures that you tackle the critical ones without procrastination.

## Step 4: Set Realistic Deadlines

Assign deadlines to each task based on their priority and the time required to complete them. Be realistic and consider the complexity and length of each task. Setting deadlines will help you stay on track and avoid last-minute rushes.

## Step 5: Break it Down

For larger tasks or projects, break them down into smaller, manageable subtasks. This approach makes the task seem less overwhelming and allows you to track your progress more effectively. By completing smaller subtasks, you'll feel a sense of accomplishment and motivation to continue working.

## Step 6: Review and Adjust

Regularly review and adjust your to-do list as needed. Life is dynamic, so unexpected events or new tasks may arise. By reviewing and adjusting your list, you can ensure that it remains relevant and reflects your current priorities.

Remember to focus on the most important tasks first and set realistic deadlines. With practice, time management will become a valuable skill that will benefit you throughout your life.

## | Achieving a Healthy School or Work-Life Balance

Imagine you're passionate about a sport or hobby, but you also have school and other responsibilities. Time management helps you strike a balance between your work and personal life. Set aside specific times for studying and completing tasks, and make sure to have designated "me" time for relaxation and doing things you love.

## | Inspiring Story

Meet Alex, a passionate gamer who absolutely loves playing video games. It wasn't uncommon for him to prioritize gaming over schoolwork, which led to a drop in his grades. He realized he needed to make a change.

Despite this, Alex decided to improve his time management skills, finding a way to balance his love for gaming and his school responsibilities. He carefully schedules time for both, ensuring that he doesn't neglect either of his passions. With his unwavering dedication to both, Alex manages to excel in both academics and gaming without sacrificing one for the other.

This newfound balance has brought a sense of fulfillment and satisfaction to Alex's life. Now, he enjoys gaming, performs well in school, and has mastered the art of time management, allowing him to live life to the fullest.

## | Valuable Insight

Time management is not about working non-stop. It's about finding a balance that allows you to be productive and still have time for fun and relaxation. By managing your time wisely, you'll have more energy for the things you love.

## | Inspiring Quote for Chapter 5

"Time management is really a misnomer - the challenge is not to manage time, but to manage ourselves." - Stephen R. Covey (A highly influential self-help and business author and speaker)

**What does this quote have to do with this chapter? Here is what this means:**

- Time management is a misnomer – the real issue is not managing time itself.
- Time will move forward steadily, no matter what we do. The key is managing ourselves and our choices.
- This quote highlights an important time management strategy, which is budgeting your time wisely.
- As a teen, you likely have a busy schedule filled with school, activities, social life, etc. It can feel overwhelming.
- But you can get more done if you plan out how to best spend your 24 hours. Prioritize your most important tasks.

- Budget time for big projects like studying for a test or writing an essay. Break it into blocks over several days vs last minute.
- Schedule time to exercise, connect with friends, and pursue hobbies, as this balances schoolwork.
- Block out specific times for tasks and stick to them. This creates structure.
- Review your schedule every Sunday to get organized and focused for the week ahead.
- Time feels limited, but budgeting removes stress. You'll see you can accomplish more.
- Don't just react to each day. Rather, be intentional with where you invest your hours.
- Master your time while you're young by creating plans. This leads to productivity and success.

Special note from the author: The key for teens is being intentional about where you put your hours and investing them wisely into growth. That's how you master time.

## | Conclusion

As we wrap up this chapter on time management, let's revisit Stephen Covey's key insight:

"*Time management is really about managing ourselves.*" I'm sure many teens often find themselves overwhelmed by their busy schedules. But you have the power to take control through self-discipline and organization. Prioritize tasks, set goals, and budget your limited time wisely. Be intentional about investing hours into meaningful activities and not just mindless distractions. Balance obligations and enjoyment. With focus and purpose, you can accomplish more than you thought possible.

Don't let time manage you; learn to manage time. Use this finite resource carefully to pursue your dreams and grow. Stay focused on channeling time into productive self-investment. You can fit everything in if you structure your days well. Have confidence in your ability to take charge of your schedule through smart time management. The future belongs to those who master themselves.

The journey through Part One has equipped you with invaluable mindsets that will shape your success and happiness — embracing challenges, believing in your ability to learn and improve, cultivating gratitude and empathy, setting ambitious goals, and time management. All these mindsets are stepping stones towards a fulfilling life.

As we transition to Part Two: Soaring Towards Greatness, get ready to explore more empowering traits and mindsets that will propel you toward an even brighter future. From proactivity and positive self-image to respecting others, staying curious, and cultivating emotional intelligence, the path to greatness is wide open.

Stay determined, stay focused, and let's soar to new heights together in Part Two! The best is yet to come, and I can't wait to witness the incredible person you'll become. Onward and upward!

# Part 2
# Soaring Towards Greatness

---

## CHAPTER 6

# EMBRACE PROACTIVITY AND INITIATIVE

✓ Being Proactive and Taking Initiative
✓ Creating Opportunities Instead of Waiting

Welcome to Chapter 6, where we'll unlock the secrets of *being proactive and taking initiative* in all aspects of life. As a teenager, you have the power to shape your own path and create opportunities that lead you toward success and fulfillment. Let's explore the incredible impact of being proactive and taking initiative and how they can elevate your journey to greatness.

## | Being Proactive and Taking Initiative

Instead of waiting for things to happen, we must go out and make them happen! Proactivity is like having a GPS guiding us toward our dreams with every decision we make. By taking initiative, we become the authors of our destiny, creating a life filled with purpose and excitement.

Sometimes, the road to our dreams might have bumps or turns we didn't expect. But by being proactive, we keep going and finding new ways to move forward. We learn from the things that don't go as planned and use those lessons to do better next time.

By choosing to be proactive, we make our lives more fun and interesting. We get to see our dreams come true because we are working towards them. It's like being the captain of a ship, steering it in the direction we want to go. We are in control, and that makes life an exciting adventure!

## | Creating Opportunities Instead of Waiting

Now that we realize that opportunities don't always knock on our doors sometimes, we must create them! Rather than waiting for the perfect moment, we must actively seek out possibilities and open doors to new experiences. By creating opportunities, we discover our hidden talents, form lasting connections, and find our true calling in life.

Like when we go on a treasure hunt, we don't just sit and wait for the treasure to find us. Rather, we go out, follow the map, dig, and discover the gold! That gold can be new friends, hobbies, jobs, or anything else that makes us happy and fulfilled. The more we search for opportunities and take chances, the more treasures we find in our lives.

Being proactive and creating opportunities means we never stop learning and growing. We become explorers of our own lives, always looking for new paths and adventures. This way, we build a life that's full of excitement, joy, and meaning, all because we chose to take charge and make things happen!

## | Teenagers Perspective

Let's say you are passionate about helping those in need. Instead of waiting for a charity organization to come to your town, you can take the initiative to start your own community service project. You can gather a group of like-minded friends, organize food drives and clothing donations, and volunteer at local shelters. Your proactivity can positively impact the lives of the less fortunate, and you inspire others in your community to join your efforts.

Or imagine you have a deep love for animals and want to create an awareness about animal welfare. Instead of waiting for someone else to address the issue, you can take the initiative to start an animal rights club at your school. With the support of your friends and classmates, you can organize events and workshops to educate others about responsible pet ownership and the importance of protecting wildlife. Your proactive approach raises awareness and fosters a compassionate community that cares for animals.

## | Practical Exercise

You know that goal you've been dreaming about? The one that tugs at your heart but seems a bit out of reach. Well, guess what? Today's the day you start turning that dream into reality. Buckle up because here's your roadmap to making it happen:

## Step 1: Define Your Dream

- First things first, jot down that goal. Make it crystal clear, like a North Star guiding you.

## Step 2: Break It Down

- Don't let its grandness overwhelm you. Break it into smaller steps, like bites of a yummy snack.

## Step 3: Set a Timeline

- Assign dates to each step. Having a timeline keeps you focused and on track.

## Step 4: Seek Guidance

- You're not alone on this journey. Don't hesitate to ask for advice or mentorship. People love to share their wisdom.

## Step 5: Surround Yourself

- Hang out with a supportive squad. Surrounding yourself with people who encourage you will keep your motivation high.

## Step 6: Track Progress

- Keep an eye on your checklist. Crossing off completed steps is like giving yourself a high-five.

## Step 7: Embrace Challenges

- Challenges? They're just tiny detours on your road to being awesome. Embrace them as learning experiences.

**Step 8: Reward Milestones**

- Celebrate! With every step you complete, treat yourself. You've earned it.

**Remember:** This journey might have bumps and curveballs, but that makes it exciting. You're the captain of your own dreams, steering toward success.

**So go ahead:** Take that first step. Whether it's signing up for a club, making that call, or starting that project, your initiative opens doors to incredible opportunities.

**Believe in yourself:** Your strength and abilities are your secret ingredients. Unleash them, and watch how your aspirations turn into accomplishments.

**You've got this:** The future you dream of? It's within reach. Ready to make it yours? Then it's time to shine!

## | Valuable Insight

Proactivity and taking the initiative are like the sparks that ignite a fire of positive change. When you take the lead and initiate action, you become a catalyst for progress and growth, not only in your life but also in the lives of those around you. Your proactive mindset sets a powerful example, inspiring others to take charge of their dreams and aspirations. It fosters a culture of empowerment and determination, where everyone is encouraged to reach their fullest potential. This ripple effect of proactive leadership echoes through communities and organizations, turning abstract ideas into tangible realities. The magic lies in the will to act, the courage to pursue, and the vision to create a better tomorrow, forging paths that others may follow. Together, we are the architects of our future, guided by a common purpose and the unyielding spirit of innovation and self-improvement.

## | Inspiring Quote for Chapter 6

"Proactivity is the key that unlocks all doors. Don't wait for the key - take the initiative to break down the door." - Tony Robbins (A renowned motivational speaker)

### What does this quote have to do with this chapter? Here is what this means:

- Proactivity means taking action before being asked or forced to.
- It's about having the initiative, drive, and determination to make things happen.
- Proactivity unlocks life's doors of opportunity, success, and growth.
- Don't sit around waiting for the keys to those doors.
- Take charge and break down those doors yourself through self-motivation.
- If you lack initiative, chances will pass you by. You must create your own chances.
- When you see an opportunity, seize it rather than wait.
- If a door is closed to you, don't accept defeat. Keep trying to open it.
- With proactivity and initiative, you can open any door you want in life.

- Refuse to take "no" for an answer. Persist until you make your own luck.
- Take the first step today to start opening doors to your dreams and goals.

Special note from the author: The key message is don't wait for things to happen automatically. Take control of your life by having the drive and determination to open doors yourself through your personal initiative.

## Conclusion

Congratulations on embracing the power of proactivity and initiative! By being proactive, you are taking charge of your life's direction and actively shaping your future. Instead of simply reacting to circumstances, you are becoming the driver of your own destiny. Proactivity is like having a compass that guides you toward your goals and dreams.

Through proactivity, you seize control of your choices and actions. You don't wait for opportunities to come knocking on your door; instead, you go out and create them. This mindset empowers you to unlock your full potential and discover your passions. When you take the initiative, you open the door to endless possibilities and pave the way to greatness.

## CHAPTER 7

# EMBRACE A POSITIVE SELF-IMAGE

✓ Developing Self-Worth: Unleashing Confidence
✓ Embracing Uniqueness: Celebrating Your Uniqueness

Welcome to Chapter 7, where we'll delve into two incredible traits—***developing a positive self-image and embracing our uniqueness* and talents**! Imagine having the power to see the best in yourself and celebrate your individuality. Well, that's exactly what these qualities do! Let's learn how to cultivate these amazing traits and become champions of self-love and self-confidence!

## Developing Self-Worth: Unleashing Confidence

Developing self-worth is like unleashing your inner confidence. It's about recognizing your value and believing in yourself. When you embrace your self-worth, you stand tall and strong, knowing that you are worthy of all the love and success that life has to offer.

This inner belief becomes a guiding force, aligning your thoughts and actions with your true self. It builds resilience and empowers you to overcome obstacles and bounce back from setbacks. With self-worth as your foundation, you approach life with a sense of purpose and integrity, understanding that you are enough as you are. You no longer seek external validation but find contentment and fulfillment in your own journey. Connections with others become more authentic as you relate with honesty and compassion.

Embracing your self-worth invites a profound transformation, unlocking a new realm of possibilities, joy, and growth. It's a lifelong commitment to yourself, a pledge to honor your unique existence, and a pathway to a life lived with passion, dignity, and grace.

## | Teenagers Perspective

Imagine a young individual who used to doubt their abilities and often felt insecure. They constantly compared themselves to others and felt inadequate. However, they decided to change their mindset and focus on their strengths and achievements. With time and practice, they began to see their worth and value. They realized that they were capable of great things and that their uniqueness was their greatest asset.

With new confidence, this young person started trying new things. They excitedly followed their interests and saw their mistakes as ways to learn and improve. Slowly, they began to feel better about themselves and encouraged others with their positive attitude toward life and their strong will.

Their journey shows that change is possible for anyone willing to take the leap. This story is a lesson to all teenagers who may be struggling with self-doubt or feeling stuck. It's a call to action to discover their potential and fully embrace themselves. By focusing on personal growth and setting achievable goals, any young person can build their self-worth and find joy in their unique path. It proves that anything is achievable with determination and a positive outlook.

## | Practical Exercise

To develop self-worth, practice daily affirmations. Look in the mirror and repeat positive statements about yourself every morning. Affirm your strengths, talents, and unique qualities. Embrace your achievements, no matter how big or small. Remember, you are worthy, capable, and deserving of happiness and success.

Here are two affirmations you can use:

1. "I am worthy of love, success, and happiness. I believe in myself and my abilities."
2. "I embrace my uniqueness and celebrate my individuality. I am confident in being true to myself."

Remember, affirmations are personal and can be tailored to suit your individual needs and preferences. The key is to create statements that resonate with you and reinforce positive beliefs about yourself. Repeat these affirmations daily, and over time, they can help boost your self-worth and confidence.

## Embracing Uniqueness: Celebrating Your Uniqueness

Embracing uniqueness is about accepting yourself as you are and knowing that your differences make you extraordinary. It's the understanding that being true to yourself is your greatest strength.

When you celebrate your uniqueness, you start to see that you don't have to be like everyone else. You realize that your own way of thinking, interests, and style make you special. You stop trying to fit into a mold and start living in a way that feels right for you.

This can make life more exciting and enjoyable. You begin to feel proud of who you are and what you can do. You may even inspire others to be themselves, too. Embracing what makes you different gives you the freedom to be yourself without worrying about what others may think.

Think of your uniqueness as a gift that only you have. It's something to be proud of and to share with the world. By being true to yourself and celebrating your differences, you can find happiness and success in ways that feel natural and right for you. It's a simple but powerful idea that can change how you see yourself and how you live your life.

## Teenagers Perspective

Imagine someone who used to try to fit in with the crowd, suppressing their unique interests and passions to avoid standing out. However, as they journeyed through self-discovery, they learned the importance of authenticity. They began to celebrate their individuality, embracing their quirks and talents.

With newfound self-acceptance, this person started to attract like-minded friends who appreciated and admired their authenticity. They stopped seeking validation from others and learned to value their own opinions and choices. Embracing their uniqueness empowered them to express their creativity freely and passionately pursue their dreams.

## | Valuable Insight

Embracing your uniqueness empowers you to navigate through life with courage and strength. When you embrace who you are, you inspire others to do the same. Celebrate your individuality and encourage others to do so as well. Remember, there is beauty in being different, and our unique qualities contribute to a rich and colorful world.

When you know and accept what makes you special, it's easier to face challenges and take risks. You don't have to pretend to be someone else or hide your true self. Instead, you can stand tall and be proud of who you are.

In a world where people often feel pressured to be the same, being yourself is a brave thing to do. It makes you a leader and a role model. By embracing your uniqueness, you show others that it's okay to be different and that there's no one "right" way to be.

This is a message that everyone can learn from, no matter their age or background. It's a reminder to trust yourself and believe in your abilities. Every person has something special to offer, and when we celebrate our differences, we make the world a more interesting and wonderful place.

## | Inspiring Quote for Chapter 7

"You are enough, you are so enough, it's unbelievable how enough you are." - Maya Angelou (A renowned poet and writer)

**What does this quote have to do with this chapter? Here is what this means:**

- You are enough just as you are. You don't need to be anyone else.
- Don't compare yourself negatively to others. You are uniquely and wonderfully you.
- Believe in yourself and your own worth. Don't question your value.
- Your flaws and mistakes don't define you. They are part of what makes you beautifully human.
- Judge yourself based on your own growth and potential, not external standards.
- Appreciate all the great qualities you have to offer the world. Have confidence in yourself.
- You are more than good enough. You are amazing just for being your true self. Never forget that.
- Don't focus on what you lack. Be proud of who you are and the person you are becoming.
- Surround yourself with people who remind you how incredible you are. Limit negative voices.
- When you embrace your worth, you're free to live boldly and authentically as your best self.

- The key message is to recognize and believe in your inherent value. Know at your core that you are absolutely enough, just as you are. Let this give you the confidence to be genuine and chase your dreams.

Special note from the author: This quote serves as a powerful reminder that you don't need to be like anyone else; "**You are already enough, just as you are.**" Embrace your uniqueness and let your authenticity shine.

## | Conclusion

This chapter taught you to love yourself and rock your unique style. In Chapter 8, you will learn to take that self-confidence and use it to respect others. When you feel good about who you are, you can also appreciate everyone else's differences. If you're proud of what makes you special, you'll be proud of what makes others special. Stand up against bullying. You know how much words can hurt when directed at you.

As you nurture acceptance of yourself, extend that openness toward people of all backgrounds. Just as you want to be appreciated for your unique identity, remember that others wish to be accepted for who they are. Seek first to understand and not judge. Suspending assumptions takes mindfulness but leads to mutually enlightening discoveries. By playing our small part with sincerity and courage, we can each create ripples that can reshape society. Embody the ideals of respect, dignity, and belonging for all, and be the change you wish to see in the world. Wherever you go, let your warm light follow. Now, let's move on to Chapter 8.

## CHAPTER 8

# RESPECTING OTHERS AND DIVERSITY

✓ Respect: The Foundation of Kindness
✓ Embracing Diversity: Celebrating Our Uniqueness

Welcome to Chapter 8, where we'll delve into two essential qualities—***respect and inclusivity***! Imagine having the power to **create a harmonious and welcoming environment for everyone** around you. That's exactly what respecting others and embracing diversity can do! These qualities foster empathy and understanding, making the world a better place for all. Let's learn how to cultivate these incredible traits and become champions of kindness and unity!

## Respect: The Foundation of Kindness

Respect is like a strong foundation on which we build our relationships and communities. It's about ***treating others with kindness and consideration, regardless of our differences***. When we practice respect, we become beacons of compassion and understanding. Let's spread this power of respect and create a world where everyone feels valued and appreciated!

## | Inspiring Story

Let me introduce you to Charles and Angela, two amazing teenagers who truly believe in standing up for others, no matter where they come from or what they believe in. One day, while they were in school, they noticed that some students were being left out and excluded from activities. They knew they couldn't just stand by and do nothing; they had to take action!

So, they both came up with a brilliant idea. They decided to start a club that promoted kindness and respect. The best part? They invited students from all walks of life to join. And guess what? The club quickly grew, and its message of inclusivity touched the hearts of many people.

Charles and Angela's respect for others created a safe and welcoming space where everyone felt accepted and celebrated. It wasn't just about saying polite words; it was about truly listening to each other and understanding that our thoughts and feelings matter. They never judged anyone based on their appearance, beliefs, or background. Instead, they embraced the uniqueness of each person, making everyone feel valued and appreciated.

You see, when we treat others with respect, we create an environment where people can freely express themselves without fear of judgment. It's like building an unbreakable bond of trust and support with the people around us. Imagine having friends who truly understand and respect you for who you are without trying to change you or put you down.

Charles and Angela's club became a shining example of how respecting others can make a real difference in people's lives. They showed us that kindness and acceptance have the power to create a more compassionate and understanding world. So, the next time you interact with someone, remember their story, and let's all strive to be more like Charles and Angela, spreading respect and love wherever we go!

## | Practical Exercise

Let's try something powerful that can shift the dynamics of your day and relationships.

Choose a day, maybe even tomorrow, to fully embrace respecting others' opinions and perspectives, especially when they're different from yours. This doesn't mean you have to agree, but genuinely listen. Understand where they're coming from without interrupting or immediately rejecting their ideas. Dive deeper by asking questions about their experiences.

You might be surprised by how this kind of respect changes things. People are likely to appreciate your willingness to understand and your open-mindedness. This isn't just about being nice; it's about growing connections and deepening your bonds with those around you.

So, is the challenge accepted? Embracing this approach, even just for a day, might show you a new way to relate to others and strengthen your relationships. And who knows, you might want to make it a regular thing. Give it a go and feel the difference!

## | Embracing Diversity: Celebrating Our Uniqueness

Diversity is like a beautiful mosaic, where each piece contributes to a vibrant and interconnected whole. When we embrace diversity, we celebrate the uniqueness of every individual. We recognize that our differences make us stronger and more resilient as a community. Let's promote unity and bridge the gaps between people, thus fostering a world of acceptance and compassion.

## | Teenager's Perspective

Embracing diversity is like unlocking the true beauty of humanity, recognizing that each person is a unique brushstroke on the canvas of life. Just as an artist carefully selects every color to create a masterpiece, we must cherish the various backgrounds, cultures, and perspectives that make us who we are.

In a world where diversity is celebrated, we find ourselves immersed in a vibrant tapestry of traditions, languages, and beliefs. We revel in the richness of different customs, savor the flavors of global cuisine, and embrace the melodies of diverse music. Each element adds depth and brilliance to the world around us, transforming it into a kaleidoscope of experiences.

When we create an atmosphere of acceptance, we provide a safe haven for everyone to express their true selves without fear of judgment. We become like a symphony, each instrument playing its unique melody yet harmonizing beautifully together. In this symphony of diversity, the beauty lies not in uniformity but in the collaboration of differences, creating a magnificent symphony of humanity.

Embracing diversity means breaking down barriers and building bridges. It's a celebration of inclusion, where every voice is heard, every story is valued, and every heart is embraced. We realize that understanding and accepting one another makes us stronger as a society, for when we stand united, we can overcome any challenge that comes our way.

As we celebrate our individuality and recognize the worth of others, we find a sense of belonging that transcends borders and unites us as a global community. In this colorful mosaic of humanity, we discover that our similarities far outweigh our differences. Just as a beautiful garden thrives with a variety of flowers, the world flourishes when we embrace diversity. The exchange of ideas and perspectives enhances our collective knowledge and empowers us to envision a better future for all.

So let us stand together, hand in hand, celebrating diversity and cherishing the uniqueness of each soul. Together, we can paint a brighter and more exciting world where love, respect, and acceptance form the foundation of our interactions. In this breathtaking masterpiece of unity, we can embrace our true selves and one another, transforming the world into a beacon of hope and possibility for generations to come.

## | Valuable Insight

Respect and inclusivity go hand in hand. When we respect others and embrace their diversity, we create an environment where everyone feels loved, safe, heard, and understood. It's like building a community that thrives on harmony and cooperation, where each person's contribution is valued and cherished.

## | Inspiring Quote for Chapter 8:

*"I have decided to stick with love. Hate is too great a burden to bear."* - Dr. Martin Luther King (A Renowned Orator, Civil Rights Leader, and Nobel Laureate)

**What does this quote have to do with this chapter? Here is what this means:**

- Hating or being prejudiced against people who aren't like you just drags you down. It's super tiring and negative. That bad energy sucks the life out of you. It's a heavy weight crushing your spirit. Instead, be positive. Keep your mindset light as a feather by staying open.
- Choosing love and respect for all people, even adversaries, lifts that burden and frees our spirit.
- Judging others negatively based on race, gender, orientation, religion, etc., divides humanity.
- Leading with love and respect unites humanity across superficial differences.
- Respecting diversity means embracing all people in their uniqueness with compassion.

- Fighting hate with more hate just breeds more bitterness and separation.
- Understanding by getting to know one another breeds empathy and brings people together.
- Respect begins by giving love and seeing the humanity in those who seem different.
- Living by unconditional love aligns with valuing the inherent worth of all people.

Special note from the author: The core message is that **cultivating love over hate** helps us respect diversity and promote inclusion. This mindset overcomes prejudice.

## | Conclusion

Congratulations on embracing the qualities of respect and inclusivity! As we move forward, let's continue spreading kindness and understanding to create a world where everyone feels valued and respected. In the next chapter, we'll explore the exciting world of curiosity and open-mindedness, where new experiences and opportunities await. It's all about staying curious, being open to learning, and adapting to new situations. Get ready to unleash your willpower and soar to new heights! Keep shining with respect and embracing diversity, and I'll see you in the next chapter!

## CHAPTER 9

# STAY CURIOUS AND OPEN-MINDED

✓ Embracing New Experiences: Discovering the Unknown
✓ Embodying Adaptability: Flexibility in the Face of Change

Welcome to Chapter 9, where we'll embark on an exciting adventure of **curiosity and open-mindedness**! Imagine having the amazing ability to explore new ideas, embrace challenges, and adapt to any situation. Well, that's exactly what curiosity and open-mindedness do! These remarkable traits unlock a world of possibilities and growth. Let's dive in and become champions of curiosity and open-mindedness!

## Embracing New Experiences: Discovering the Unknown

Embracing new experiences through curiosity is like having a magical treasure map that leads us to fascinating discoveries. It's about being excited to learn and explore unfamiliar territories. Just like adventurous explorers, curiosity drives us to uncover the wonders of knowledge and understanding.

When we practice curiosity, we become like detectives, constantly seeking clues and answers to our questions. It sparks our imagination and ignites a thirst for learning that knows no bounds. By being curious, we open doors to new possibilities and expand our horizons beyond what we previously thought possible.

Imagine encountering something you've never seen before, like a rare species of flower or an ancient artifact. Curiosity encourages you to investigate further, unraveling the mysteries of the world around you. This eagerness to learn fuels a sense of wonder and amazement, making life an exciting journey of constant discovery.

Curiosity is not limited to external exploration; it also fuels self-discovery. By being curious about ourselves, we delve into our passions, strengths, and weaknesses, understanding who we truly are. This inner journey of self-discovery helps us grow and become more self-aware, leading to personal development and fulfillment.

As we embrace curiosity, we develop an insatiable appetite for knowledge, always seeking to learn more and understand better. It keeps us engaged and motivated, turning each day into a thrilling adventure filled with opportunities for growth and enlightenment.

Let's celebrate the gift of curiosity and cherish it as a valuable companion in our journey through life. By being curious, we remain open to the wonders of the unknown, ready to explore and experience the richness that the world has to offer. So, let's be like adventurers of knowledge, embarking on exciting journeys of learning, self-discovery, and wonder. Embrace curiosity, and let it guide us toward a life full of exploration and fulfillment!

## Teenager's Perspective

Imagine you have a friend who's passionate about playing the guitar. They invite you to join their band, but you've never played an instrument before. Instead of hesitating, you embrace curiosity and decide to give it a try. You attend band practice twice weekly, learn to strum the chords, and now you are playing your favorite songs together. Your curiosity led you to uncover a hidden talent and forge new friendships! It's amazing how trying something new can lead to wonderful experiences and opportunities.

## Practical Exercise

Ready to flex those curiosity muscles? Then let's dive into the "Curiosity Challenge".

Choose something you've always wondered about. Maybe it's a dance move you've seen online, a language spoken in a movie, or the wonders of outer space. Now's your time to dig deeper.

Dedicate a bit of your day to explore this new territory. You can watch videos, read articles, or even chat with experts in the field. And don't stress about mastering it; this is all about the journey and the fun of discovery.

You know what's cool? You'll probably find that the more you explore, the more you'll want to know. Curiosity has a way of lighting up our brains and introducing us to passions we never knew we had.

So, are you up for the challenge? Dive in, get curious, and watch as new worlds open up before you. The universe is full of wonders, and your next obsession could be just one search away. Dive in and let curiosity lead the way!

## Embodying Adaptability: Flexibility in the Face of Change

Embodying adaptability through open-mindedness is like having a versatile tool that helps us navigate through the ever-changing world. It's about being open to new ideas and perspectives and being willing to adjust our thoughts and beliefs when faced with new information. Just like chameleons change their colors to blend with their surroundings, open-mindedness allows us to adapt and understand different situations and people better.

When we practice open-mindedness, we become more receptive to others' opinions and experiences, breaking down barriers that may have hindered understanding and cooperation. It creates an environment of inclusivity and fosters unity among people with diverse backgrounds and beliefs.

Moreover, open-mindedness is a bridge to celebrating the diversity of thoughts and cultures around us. It allows us to appreciate the beauty of varied perspectives and traditions, fostering a sense of harmony and respect for one another.

As we face the dynamic nature of life, open-mindedness becomes a valuable asset. It empowers us to adapt to change with grace and curiosity instead of fear or resistance. Just as a versatile tool has various applications, open-mindedness equips us to approach different situations with flexibility and understanding.

Let's celebrate the power of open-mindedness by actively incorporating it into our lives. By doing so, we can build a world that embraces diversity and thrives on unity, making it a better place for everyone. Embrace adaptability, embrace open-mindedness, and let it guide us on a journey of continuous learning and growth.

## | Teenager's Perspective

Imagine you and your friends are planning a fun day out, and everyone has different ideas on what to do. Instead of sticking to your own suggestion, you embody open-mindedness. You listen to your friends' ideas, weigh the options, and choose an activity that everyone can enjoy together. Embodying open-mindedness strengthens relationships and promotes a sense of belonging.

## | Practical Exercise

This simple challenge will help you level up your conversation skills.

Next time you're chatting with friends or family, try giving them your full attention – like, really tune in. It's about letting them share their stories, opinions, or whatever's on their mind without jumping in with judgments or distractions.

Do you have a curious streak? Perfect! Use it to ask questions. Dive deeper into what they're saying. It's not just about being polite; it's about genuinely wanting to know more.

And guess what? Being open-minded in these conversations does something awesome: it strengthens your bond. You'll be surprised how much more you connect with them when you really listen and stay curious.

Ready to give it a shot? The next chat you have, dive in with both ears and an open heart. Let's make those connections count!

## | Valuable Insight

Curiosity and open-mindedness make an awesome team. When we stay curious, we're like detectives, always ready to explore and discover new things. And being open-minded means we're cool with hearing other people's ideas and perspectives, even if they're different from ours. It's like a secret passageway to constant learning and becoming better versions of ourselves! So, let's keep our curiosity alive and our minds open for all the amazing insights waiting to be uncovered!

## | **Inspiring Quote for Chapter 9:**

"I have not failed. I've just found 10,000 ways that won't work."
– Thomas Edison (A highly prolific American inventor)

- Edison tried 10,000 different materials for the lightbulb filament before finding one that worked.
- He didn't see those 10,000 unsuccessful tries as failures. To him, they were lessons.
- If he had given up after a few attempts, he would never have succeeded. Persistence matters.
- He stayed endlessly curious to find solutions. He knew success was just one more try away.
- When you're curious, you don't dwell on setbacks. Rather, you're excited to try new approaches.
- Failure is feedback that teaches you what doesn't work so that you get smarter.
- An open mindset sees opportunities in obstacles. Curiosity pushes you to keep trying.
- Don't let roadblocks stop your curiosity. Stay positive and try new angles.
- Keep asking questions, experimenting, and exploring without fear of failure.
- Curiosity combined with grit leads to breakthroughs. Stay relentlessly curious!

Special note from the author: Edison showed that curiosity powers persistence through challenges. Maintain an open and positive mindset, focused on growth and discovery.

## | Conclusion

Congratulations on embracing curiosity and open-minded-ness—the empowering traits of learning and understanding! As we journey forward, let's continue exploring new horizons and celebrating different perspectives. Curiosity leads us to in-credible discoveries, while open-mindedness fosters unity and acceptance. In the next chapter, we'll delve into the im-portance of emotional intelligence and self-awareness. Get ready to tap into your emotions and connect with others on a deeper level. Keep the spirit of curiosity and open-mindedness alive, and I'll see you in the next and final chapter!

## CHAPTER 10

# CULTIVATE EMOTIONAL INTELLIGENCE (THE BIG ONE)

✓ Developing Emotional Intelligence: The Key to Understanding Yourself
✓ Understanding and Effectively Managing Emotions: Nurturing Empathy and Compassion
✓ The Importance of Emotional Intelligence in Everyday Life
✓ The Impact of Emotional Intelligence on Leadership and Success
✓ The Journey of Lifelong Growth

Welcome to the final and most transformative chapter of our epic journey! In Chapter 10, we will deeply explore a game-changing trait—***emotional intelligence (EQ)***. This is the big one. This mindset will shape your path to success and happiness like no other. Emotional intelligence is like a secret treasure hidden within you, waiting to be discovered and unlocked. It's all about understanding yourself, connecting with others, and navigating through life's challenges with grace and empathy. Let's dive deep, I mean deep into the world of emotional intelligence, and become true masters of self-awareness and compassion!

## Developing Emotional Intelligence: The Key to Understanding Yourself

Emotional intelligence (EQ) is not just an abstract concept—it's the key to unlocking your true self. It's about recognizing your feelings, strengths, and areas for growth. This trait empowers you to become a wise observer of your own emotions, thoughts, and behaviors. By developing emotional intelligence, you become attuned to the language of your heart, making better decisions and building fulfilling relationships.

An incredible aspect of emotional intelligence is how it empowers us to handle conflicts and disagreements with finesse. We've all been in situations where tensions rise, and arguments flare up like fireworks. But with emotional intelligence, we can be like peacemakers, defusing the situation with empathy and understanding. It's like having a magic wand that turns conflicts into opportunities for growth and connection.

And you know what? Emotional intelligence also makes us better decision-makers. When we're aware of our emotions and how they influence our choices, it's like having a supercomputer that calculates the best course of action. We can step back and evaluate situations clearly, weighing the pros and cons before making choices. It's like having a crystal ball that shows us the potential outcomes, helping us make choices we won't regret.

As we continue our quest to cultivate emotional intelligence, let's not forget about self-compassion. It's easy to be hard on ourselves when we make mistakes or face challenges. But with emotional intelligence, we become like our own best friends, offering kindness and understanding when we stumble. It's like having an inner cheerleader that motivates us to keep going, even when the going gets tough.

Moreover, emotional intelligence enriches our connections with others. It's like having a special pair of glasses that allows us to see beyond the surface and truly understand what someone is going through. When our friends or family share their feelings, we can be like heart-listeners, lending a supportive ear without judgment. We become like the glue that holds relationships together, thus fostering trust and intimacy.

## | Teenager's Perspective

Picture yourself in a situation where you have to make a crucial decision about your future. You find yourself torn between following your heart's passion or opting for a more practical path that others may deem safer. It's a challenging moment, and you feel the weight of this decision on your shoulders.

But instead of pushing your emotions aside, you decide to apply emotional intelligence. You take in a deep breath and step back to give yourself space to think and feel. You understand that emotions play a significant role in making decisions, and it's essential to acknowledge them.

So, you take the time to listen to your inner feelings. What does your heart truly yearn for? What sparks that fire of excitement within you? On the other hand, what are your fears and concerns about choosing the more practical path?

Through this process of self-awareness, you start to gain clarity. You realize that deep down, you have a passion and a dream that you've always wanted to pursue. It's something that aligns perfectly with your values and aspirations. Your heart tells you that following this path would bring you genuine fulfillment.

On the other hand, you also acknowledge the practical concerns and the opinions of those around you. It's not easy to ignore the potential challenges that come with pursuing your passion. But with emotional intelligence, you understand that the decision isn't just about what others think is right; it's about what feels right to you.

So, armed with this newfound self-awareness, you make your decision. You choose to follow your heart and pursue your passion, knowing that it might not be the easiest path, but it's the one that feels authentic and fulfilling to you.

In the end, applying emotional intelligence leads you to a decision that is genuinely yours—a decision that empowers you to embrace your dreams and aspirations wholeheartedly. It's a decision that will shape your future and set you on a path of passion and purpose. So, the next time you face a tough decision, remember the power of emotional intelligence and trust yourself to make the best choice for your unique journey.

## | Practical Exercise

Practice mindfulness and self-awareness every day. Take a few minutes to check in with your emotions, thoughts, and physical sensations. Use a journal to jot down your feelings and reflect on your experiences. The more you develop emotional intelligence, the more you'll understand your true self.

Exercise Example:

- Set aside five minutes each day for self-reflection. Find a quiet space.
- Check in on your emotions – what are you feeling? Happy? Irritated? Nervous?
- Notice any physical sensations — tense shoulders? Butterflies in your stomach?
- Observe your thoughts — are they anxious, optimistic, or judgmental?
- Ask why you feel and think this way. What experiences or triggers caused this?
- Consider if your feelings/thoughts serve you or not. Do they motivate or distract you?
- Resist the urge to suppress unpleasant emotions. Accept them with self-kindness.
- Write down your reflections in a journal and look for patterns over time.
- Share your feelings with a trusted friend. Ask for their observations about your emotions.
- Before reacting to situations, pause and check in with yourself first.
- Developing self-awareness takes practice but builds emotional intelligence over time. Be patient with yourself!

## Understanding and Effectively Managing Emotions: Nurturing Empathy and Compassion

Emotional intelligence is not only about understanding yourself; it's also the bridge that connects you to others. It's the art of understanding their feelings, showing empathy, and offering support. When you understand and manage your emotions, you become like a beacon of compassion, spreading kindness and understanding to everyone around you.

## Teenager's Perspective

Now, let's shift gears and imagine a different scenario. You're at school, and during a break, you notice one of your classmates sitting alone, looking visibly upset. Many might choose to ignore the situation and carry on with their day, but you decide to apply emotional intelligence and show genuine care for this person.

With kindness in your heart, you approach your classmate and ask if everything is okay. Your genuine concern shines through, making them feel seen and valued. You lend a listening ear, allowing them the space to share their thoughts and feelings without judgment.

Your act of empathy and support makes a significant impact on their day. They feel understood and appreciated, knowing that someone cared enough to reach out and offer a helping hand. Your simple act of compassion helps them feel less alone and more connected.

In moments like these, emotional intelligence shines as a powerful tool in building meaningful connections with others. It reminds us of the importance of being there for each other and showing kindness and empathy even when we don't fully understand what someone might be going through.

By employing emotional intelligence, you become a beacon of support for those around you. You create a positive ripple effect in your school community, making it a warmer and more understanding place for everyone.

So, the next time you come across someone who seems upset or in need of a listening ear, remember the impact your empathy can have. Your small act of kindness might make a world of difference in someone's day and let them know that they matter and are cared for. Let's continue to cultivate emotional intelligence and spread compassion wherever we go.

## | Practical Exercise

Empathy is all about understanding other people's feelings and responding with kindness. It helps you connect with friends, family, and even strangers. This exercise is a simple guide to practicing empathy in your everyday life. Follow these steps, you can become a more compassionate friend and family member and also make a positive impact in your community. It's a skill that makes you feel good and helps others feel understood and cared for, too! Let's get started.

### 1. Understand Emotions

- Talk about your feelings with friends.
- Guess people's emotions by looking at their faces.
- Write down your own feelings sometimes.

## 2. Try Role-Playing

- Act out different situations with friends.
- Talk about how it felt afterward.

## 3. Listen and Validate

- Listen to friends without interrupting.
- Let them know you understand their feelings.

## 4. Volunteer

- Help out in your community.
- Think about how it makes others feel.

## 5. Be Kind

- Do something nice for someone, like holding a door.
- Tell a friend about it.

## 6. Be Nice Online

- Treat people online as you would in person.

## 7. Spend Time with Family and Friends

- Understand each other's feelings.
- Help a friend if they need it.

## Remember:

- Keep practicing every day.
- Ask for help if you need it.
- Think about how you're doing and be proud of yourself.

By following these steps, you'll learn how to understand others better and be a kinder person. It's cool, and it makes a difference!

## The Importance of Emotional Intelligence in Everyday Life

Emotional intelligence is not something you save for special occasions; it's a powerful tool you can use every single day. No matter what life throws your way, emotional intelligence will be there to guide you through it all. When conflicts arise and things get tough, emotional intelligence empowers you to handle them with grace and compassion. Instead of reacting impulsively, you can respond thoughtfully, considering the emotions of others and finding constructive solutions.

In the face of challenges, emotional intelligence gives you the inner strength and understanding to stay resilient. You can manage your emotions and remain focused on finding ways to overcome obstacles with confidence. As you form new relationships, emotional intelligence becomes the key to building strong connections with others. By listening, empathizing, and understanding, you can create bonds based on trust and mutual respect.

Life is full of complexities, but with emotional intelligence as your guiding light, you can navigate through them with confidence and understanding. It becomes a reliable compass that helps you make decisions aligned with your values and aspirations. So, embrace emotional intelligence as an essential tool in your daily life. Let it be your constant companion in dealing with conflicts, facing challenges, and forming meaningful relationships. As you cultivate this trait, you'll find yourself becoming more self-aware, empathetic, and resilient—a powerful combination that will lead you to a life filled with purpose, happiness, and success.

## | Teenager's Perspective

Let's examine another scenario that you might encounter in your life. Imagine you have a disagreement with your best friend. In the heat of the moment, you feel anger bubbling up inside you, but you decide to take a different approach and apply emotional intelligence. Instead of letting your anger take control, you take a deep breath and compose yourself. You realize that emotions can sometimes cloud your judgment and want to handle the situation with care and empathy. You then decide to express your feelings calmly and honestly to your best friend. You share how their actions or words have affected you without apportioning blame or becoming defensive. This open and respectful communication allows your friend to understand your perspective better. But you don't stop there. You also take the time to listen to your friend's perspective. You genuinely want to understand their point of view and what led to the disagreement. By actively listening, you show that you value their feelings and experiences.

Through this exchange of emotions and perspectives, something incredible happens. Empathy and understanding bridge the gap between you and your best friend. You both begin to see the situation from each other's point of view, and a sense of connection and closeness emerges.

With emotional intelligence guiding the way, you both work together to find a resolution that suits both of you. Perhaps it's finding a compromise, apologizing, or simply agreeing to let go of the issue. Whatever the outcome, it brings you closer together, thus strengthening the bond you share.

In this scenario, emotional intelligence becomes the key to preserving and nurturing your friendship. Instead of letting the anger and conflict escalate, you choose empathy, understanding, and open communication. The result is a stronger and more resilient friendship that can weather any storm.

Remember, conflicts are a natural part of any relationship, but how we handle them can make all the difference. By applying emotional intelligence, you can navigate through disagreements with grace and compassion, building stronger connections with the people you care about most. So, embrace emotional intelligence as a powerful tool in your relationships, and watch how it can transform your interactions for the better!

## Practical Exercise

In our day-to-day lives, it's so easy to get caught up in the whirlwind of emotions. However, pause and breathe before letting those emotions take the driver's seat. Remember, understanding your emotions and those of others (a.k.a. emotional intelligence) can lead to way cooler convos and even stronger friendships. Check out this routine to level up your emotional game:

## Daily Emotional Intelligence Routine

### 1. Tune into Your Feelings

a. **Morning Vibes:** Every morning, maybe while brushing your teeth or having breakfast, ask yourself, "How am I feeling today?"

b. **Mid-day Check:** Set phone reminders. Maybe after every class or during lunch breaks to see what's happening inside. Are you stressed about a test? Excited about a weekend plan?

## 2. Take a Chill Pill

a. **The 5-Second Rule:** Before snapping or saying something you might regret, count to five in your head.

b. **Breathe Easy:** Feeling overwhelmed? Take in three deep breaths. Trust me; it can change the game.

## 3. Get in Their Sneakers

a. Imagine being in the other person's place. It could help you understand why they acted a certain way.

b. Everyone's fighting a battle you know nothing about. So, maybe that rude comment wasn't about you but something they're going through.

## 4. Listen and Respond with Care

a. **True Listening:** Give peeps your full attention. (Yes, that means putting your phone down for a second 😊)

b. Even if you disagree, a simple "I get where you're coming from" can make someone's day.

## 5. Night-time Rewind

a. Before hitting the bed, think about your day. Are there any convos you wish went differently? Are there any proud, emotional moments?

b. Celebrate your wins, and don't beat yourself up over the oops moments. Tomorrow's another chance!

### 6. Diary or Notes App

a. Jot down tricky situations and how you felt. This isn't homework; it's for you to spot trends and grow.

b. Highlight the times you were super proud of handling things emotionally.

### 7. Feedback? Yes, please!

a. Ask your close pals: "Hey, was I too snappy today?" or "Did I handle that chat well?" Their insights might surprise you!

### 8. Never Stop Learning

a. Read or watch stuff on understanding emotions. There are some fab YouTubers, bloggers, and books out there.

b. Join clubs or groups at school that focus on communication, debate, or even theater. They help more than you think.

Remember, nobody's perfect. Even if you have a day where your emotions feel like a rollercoaster, it's all part of the journey. Keep going, and navigating through the emotional waves will soon become second nature!

## The Impact of Emotional Intelligence on Leadership and Success

Emotional intelligence is essential in personal relationships and an incredibly powerful tool for leaders and high achievers. When you cultivate emotional intelligence, it opens up a world of opportunities to connect deeply with others and create a positive impact in various aspects of your life.

For leaders, emotional intelligence is like a superpower. It allows you to understand your team members' emotions and needs, enabling you to inspire trust and collaboration. When your team feels heard, valued, and understood, they become more motivated and engaged in their work. This, in turn, leads to improved productivity and creativity within the group.

As a leader with high emotional intelligence, you can navigate through challenges with empathy and grace. You can build strong relationships with your team members, fostering a sense of belonging and loyalty. When your team feels supported and cared for, they become more willing to go the extra mile and invest in the success of the collective.

Moreover, emotional intelligence helps leaders make well-informed decisions. By understanding the emotions and perspectives of those involved, you can weigh the potential impact of your choices more effectively. This enables you to make decisions that benefit both the organization and the individuals within it, creating a win-win situation.

Leaders who prioritize emotional intelligence create positive and supportive environments where everyone thrives. They encourage open communication, collaboration, and mutual respect, fostering a culture of growth and development. In such environments, team members feel safe to express their ideas, take risks, and learn from their mistakes without fear of judgment.

High achievers also benefit greatly from emotional intelligence. When you possess emotional intelligence, you can manage your emotions effectively, staying calm and composed even in high-pressure situations. This allows you to stay focused on your goals and overcome obstacles with resilience and determination.

Furthermore, emotional intelligence enhances your ability to understand and empathize with the emotions of those around you. This can be incredibly valuable in networking, negotiation, and building strong professional relationships. Your capacity to connect with others on an emotional level can open doors and lead to meaningful collaborations and opportunities.

In conclusion, emotional intelligence is a superpower that empowers leaders and high achievers to make a positive change and cultivate supportive environments. Leaders can inspire trust, collaboration, and well-informed decision-making by understanding and connecting with others emotionally. With emotional intelligence as a guiding force, leaders and high achievers can pave the way for success and make a lasting impact in their personal and professional endeavors.

## | Teenager's Perspective

Let's picture a scenario where you're leading a school project, and your team encounters some disagreements and conflicts. It can be challenging to handle such situations, but here's where emotional intelligence comes to the rescue!

Instead of trying to boss everyone around or exert authority, you decide to apply emotional intelligence. You take a step back and listen to each team member's ideas and concerns with an open mind. By doing this, you show them that their opinions and contributions truly matter.

When conflicts arise, you don't ignore them or let them escalate. Instead, you step in as a mediator with empathy and understanding. You try to see things from everyone's perspective, helping them find common ground and solutions that work for everyone.

Your approach creates a positive and supportive atmosphere within the team. Everyone feels heard, respected, and valued. This boosts their motivation and commitment to the project because they know their voices are being heard.

As a result, your team becomes more motivated and starts working together with renewed enthusiasm. They are willing to put in their best efforts because they believe in the project's success.

With emotional intelligence guiding the way, your team overcomes the challenges, and the project's success soars. Your ability to handle conflicts with empathy and encourage everyone's input has made all the difference.

So, remember, being a great leader isn't about bossing people around; it's about connecting with your team emotionally, understanding their feelings, and creating an environment where everyone can thrive. When you apply emotional intelligence, you can inspire and lead your team to achieve amazing things together!

## | Practical Exercise

In group dynamics or when you find yourself in a leadership position, it's not just about what you say but how well you listen and understand your team members. Here's a quick guide on how to lead effectively with emotional intelligence:

### 1. Active Listening

- **Tune In:** Focus completely on the speaker. This isn't just about hearing their words but truly understanding their message.
- **Avoid Interruptions:** Resist the urge to interject or give your opinion immediately. Let them finish their thoughts.

### 2. Show Empathy

- **Acknowledge Feelings:** Recognize and validate people's emotions. A simple "I can see how you'd feel that way" can make a huge difference.
- **Understand Perspectives:** Always try to understand where others are coming from, even if you don't necessarily agree.

### 3. Promote Open Communication

- **Encourage Voices:** Make sure everyone feels their input is valuable. Sometimes, those with the quietest voices have the most profound things to say.
- **Ask Open-Ended Questions:** Encourage deeper thinking and discussion by asking questions that can't be answered with just a 'yes' or 'no.'

## 4. Create a Safe Space

- **Respect Opinions:** Even if there are disagreements, it's essential to ensure that everyone feels their views are respected.
- **Avoid Judgment:** Remember that everyone has different experiences and backgrounds that shape their opinions.

Practicing these principles will establish you as a trusted and effective leader and inspire others in the group. When you lead with emotional intelligence, you invite everyone to bring their best selves forward, making the entire group more collaborative and productive.

## | The Journey of Lifelong Growth

Emotional intelligence is not something you achieve and then forget about; it's an ongoing journey of growth and development. As you nurture and cultivate this trait, you'll experience remarkable changes in yourself and your interactions with others.

Imagine it as a path of self-discovery and understanding. As you become more emotionally intelligent, you understand your emotions better and become more aware of how they affect your thoughts and actions. This self-awareness empowers you to make better decisions and respond more effectively to life's challenges.

But that's not all! Emotional intelligence also transforms how you relate to others. You become more empathetic and understanding, putting yourself in someone else's shoes and genuinely connecting with their feelings. This deep connection strengthens your relationships and fosters a sense of trust and support among your friends, family, and colleagues.

Emotional intelligence becomes your reliable compass through the twists and turns of life. It guides you to make choices that align with your values and aspirations, leading you toward a path of meaning, happiness, and fulfillment. You'll find that you make decisions that bring you closer to your goals and contribute positively to the lives of those around you.

The journey of developing emotional intelligence is incredibly rewarding. It's a process of growth that never truly ends, as there's always room to deepen your understanding and expand your emotional skills. With each step you take on this journey, you'll notice positive changes in how you handle emotions, communicate with others, and navigate through the complexities of life.

So, embrace the journey of emotional intelligence and let it be your guiding light toward personal growth and more fulfilling relationships. As you continue to develop this invaluable trait, you'll live a more enriched and purposeful life, positively impacting yourself and the world around you.

## Teenager's Perspective

Imagine you encounter setbacks and disappointments in your journey. Instead of feeling defeated, you apply emotional intelligence. You embrace your emotions, learn from experiences, and focus on growth. With resilience and empathy, you transform challenges into stepping stones toward your dreams.

## | Practical Exercise

Committing to developing your emotional intelligence is like sharpening a valuable skill that will serve you in various aspects of life. Here's a step-by-step guide to help you navigate through this journey:

### 1. Lifelong Commitment

- **Consistency:** Emotional intelligence is about consistent effort and understanding. It's a continuous journey, not a destination.

### 2. Seek Feedback

- **Reach Out:** Ask friends, family, or trusted mentors about how you handle emotions and interpersonal situations.
- **Listen Actively:** While it can be challenging to hear feedback at times, approach it with an open mind, aiming to grow.

### 3. Embrace Challenges

- **Growth Moments:** Every difficult situation or misunderstanding offers a chance to refine your emotional skills.
- **Reflect:** After confronting an issue, evaluate what went well and what you could've approached differently.

## 4. Compassion is Key

- **For Others:** Strive to understand and respect others' feelings and viewpoints. This not only enriches your relationships but also broadens your perspective.
- **For Yourself:** Everyone makes mistakes. Instead of dwelling on them, focus on learning and growing. Treat yourself with the same understanding and kindness you'd offer a friend.

As you continue on this path, remember that the goal isn't perfection. It's about cultivating better self-awareness, enhancing your relationships, and responding to situations with insight and maturity. This journey will undoubtedly shape you into a more understanding and empathetic individual.

## | Inspiring Quote for Chapter 10:

"Emotional intelligence, the key to success, enables us to build relationships, communicate effectively, and make better decisions. It can be learned and developed through practice." – Charles Tyler (Your friend, Lifelong learner, and Educator)

**What does this quote have to do with this chapter? Here is what this means:**

- **Emotional Intelligence as the Key to Success**: The quote underscores that emotional intelligence (EQ) is vital in achieving success in different areas of life.
- **Building Relationships**: EQ plays a significant role in forming and maintaining meaningful relationships with others. It implies that understanding and managing emotions are essential for building connections.

- **Effective Communication**: EQ is linked to effective communication. It suggests that being emotionally aware and sensitive helps in conveying messages more clearly and empathetically.
- **Better Decision-Making**: The quote indicates that a high EQ contributes to making better decisions. The ability to recognize and regulate one's emotions and those of others can enable one to make wiser decisions.
- **Learnable and Developable Skill**: The quote emphasizes that emotional intelligence is not innate but can be acquired and improved through practice and learning, suggesting that personal growth is attainable.

Special note from the author: Learn to understand and manage your emotions, as they greatly impact your thoughts and actions. Develop empathy by listening to others' perspectives with an open mind and heart. Choose optimism and resilience to overcome life's inevitable challenges and thrive.

## | Conclusion

Congratulations on completing this extraordinary journey of self-discovery and personal growth! In Chapter 10, we delved deep into the world of emotional intelligence—the big mindset that transforms lives and shapes destinies. By developing emotional intelligence and self-awareness, you have unlocked the power to understand yourself better and connect with others empathetically. You are now equipped with the tools to navigate life's challenges, form deep and meaningful relationships, and become a remarkable leader.

As you continue your journey through life, remember that emotional intelligence is not just a trait—it's a way of living. Embrace the wisdom of understanding your emotions, the magic of empathy, and the power of compassion. These qualities will elevate you to new heights and guide you toward success, happiness, and fulfillment.

I am in awe of the extraordinary person you are becoming. Your journey doesn't end here; it's just the beginning of a life filled with purpose and impact. I can't wait to see you accomplish remarkable feats and make the world a better place.

As you go forth, embrace the mindsets and concepts discussed in this book, carry them in your heart, and share them with others. Your journey is bound to inspire and uplift those around you, just as it has inspired and uplifted me.

So, as we close this chapter, remember you are the author of your own story—the master of your destiny. With emotional intelligence as your guide, you hold the pen to write a life filled with love, kindness, and extraordinary achievements.

Onward and upward, my friend. I look forward to one day reading about you in magazines or seeing you on TV, sharing your incredible impact on the world by embracing the mindsets and concepts discussed in this book. Your journey is destined for greatness, and I am here cheering you on every step of the way. Keep shining, growing, and embracing the extraordinary spirit within you. The world awaits your brilliance!

Now, as an instructor, I have an assignment for you.

## | Your Assignment:

I invite you to embark on a research journey into the remarkable individuals quoted in this book. Please take this opportunity to deeply examine their extraordinary lives and their profound impact on society as we know it. By learning more about these exceptional individuals, you will gain valuable insights into the mindsets and principles that guided them toward greatness.

As you explore their stories, reflect on how their experiences align with the mindsets discussed in this book. Look for instances where their determination, empathy, resilience, or proactivity played a crucial role in their achievements. Consider how their positive self-image and openness to new experiences contributed to their success.

Furthermore, take note of how these extraordinary individuals overcame challenges and setbacks. Examine the ways they managed their emotions and harnessed emotional intelligence to navigate through difficult times. By understanding their journeys, you may find inspiration and wisdom that can guide you on your own path to greatness.

This research assignment is not just about learning facts; it's about gaining a deeper understanding of the human spirit and the limitless potential within each of us. As you uncover the stories of these remarkable individuals, think about how their lessons can be applied to your life. How can their experiences and mindset concepts empower you to overcome obstacles, embrace diversity, and create a positive impact in your community?

Remember, you, too, have the power to make a difference in the world. By studying the lives of these extraordinary individuals, you will discover that greatness is not reserved for a select few but is within reach of anyone who embraces the right mindsets and principles. So, immerse yourself in this research assignment, and let the stories of these exceptional individuals inspire you to reach new heights and make a lasting impact in your own life and the lives of others. Your journey to greatness has just begun!

## | Full disclosure:

The quote by Eleanor Roosevelt in the introduction page, "*The future belongs to those who believe in the beauty of their dreams,*" was an excellent choice for the introductory page of this book, "*10 Mindsets to Embrace Teenage Success, Happiness, and a Determined Path in Life.*" Here's why:

1. **Inspiration**: The quote is highly inspirational and sets a positive and motivating tone for the entire book. I am confident it will encourage readers, especially you as teenagers, to believe in your dreams and the possibilities that lie ahead.

2. **Empowerment**: By emphasizing that the future belongs to those who believe in their dreams, the quote empowers young readers like you to take charge of their lives and pursue their aspirations with determination and confidence.

3. **Relevance**: I believe the quote is directly relevant to the themes and content of this book, which focuses on empowering you as teenagers with the right mindsets to

achieve success and happiness in life. It aligns with the core message of the book.

4. **Connection to Adolescence**: Adolescence is a critical phase where young individuals like you explore their dreams, passions, and ambitions. Eleanor Roosevelt's quote resonates with your age group, encouraging you to hold onto your dreams and work towards making them a reality.

5. **Timelessness**: To me, the quote by Eleanor Roosevelt is timeless and has universal appeal. It transcends generations and remains relevant to teenagers of any era, making it a timeless piece of wisdom.

6. **Recognizable Source**: Eleanor Roosevelt was a highly influential figure in history, known for her advocacy of human rights and her powerful quotes. Using a quote from such a prominent and respected figure adds credibility and authority to the message of this book, I think.

In conclusion, Eleanor Roosevelt's quote, "*The future belongs to those who believe in the beauty of their dreams,*" serves as an inspirational and relevant opening for this book. It sets the right tone and encourages teenagers like yourself to embrace your dreams, have confidence in yourself, and be open to the transformative power of the mindsets shared in this book.

# RESOURCES

**Articles, Websites, and Other Resources That Inspired Each Chapter:**

## Chapter 1

Oregon State University. (2019, August 19th). Growth Mindset: What it is, and how to cultivate one., from https://success.oregonstate.edu/learning/growth-mindset

Today.com. (2020, February 1st). Supporting Teens' Curiosity: Here's What to Know. https://www.today.com/parenting-guides/supporting-teens-curiosity-t179077

Vyas, D. (2022, April 7th). Guide to Developing Growth Mindset for Teens. LinkedIn. https://www.linkedin.com/pulse/guide-developing-growth-mindset-teens-deepali-vyas

## Chapter 2

Harvard Business Review. (2018, May 31st). The Right Way to Respond to Negative Feedback. https://hbr.org/2018/05/the-right-way-to-respond-to-negative-feedback

The Muse. (2020, June 19th). How Smart People Respond to Constructive Criticism. https://www.themuse.com/advice/taking-constructive-criticism-like-a-champ

Connections Academy. (2023, February 23rd). How Students Can Accept Criticism and Grow from Feedback. https://www.connectionsacademy.com/support/resources/article/how-students-can-accept-criticism-and-grow-from-feedback/

## Chapter 3

Greater Good Science Center. (2015, June 30th). Four Great Gratitude Strategies. https://greatergood.berkeley.edu/article/item/four_great_gratitude_strategies

Greater Good Science Center. (2017, June 6th). How Gratitude Changes You and Your Brain. https://greatergood.berkeley.edu/article/item/how_gratitude_changes_you_and_your_brain

Greater Good Science Center. (2017, November 15th). How to Teach Gratitude to Tweens and Teens. https://greatergood.berkeley.edu/article/item/how_to_teach_gratitude_to_tweens_and_teens

## Chapter 4

Duckworth, A. L. (2013, April 30th). Grit: The power of passion and perseverance [Video]. TED. https://www.ted.com/talks/angela_lee_duckworth_grit_the_power_of_passion_and_perseverance?language=en

Dweck, C. S. (2019, March 26th). The power of determination. Psychology Today. https://www.psychologytoday.com/us/blog/what-mentally-strong-people-dont-do/201903/the-power-determination

Verywell Family. (2020, April 17th). 7 Steps Parents Can Take to Teach Kids Grit. https://www.verywellfamily.com/how-parents-can-teach-kids-grit-4126106

## Chapter 5:

Verywell Family. (2019, November 8th). How to Teach Time Management Skills to Teens. https://www.verywellfamily.com/teaching-time-management-skills-to-teens-2608794

Life Skills Advocate. (2022, February 3rd). 13 Practical Time Management Skills To Teach Teens. https://lifeskillsadvocate.com/blog/13-practical-time-management-skills-to-teach-teens/

E-Tutoring. (2022, November 29th). Time management for teens. https://ectutoring.com/time-management-for-teens

## Chapter 6

Deurlein, R. (2017, September 30th). Teaching kids to be proactive. https://rebeccadeurlein.wordpress.com/2017/09/30/teaching-kids-to-be-proactive/

**Roots of Action.** (2018, June 20th). Take initiative, kids! https://www.rootsofaction.com/take-initiative-kids/

## Chapter 7

Big Life Journal. (2023). 15 Tips to Build Self Esteem and Confidence in Teens. https://biglifejournal.com/blogs/blog/build-self-esteem-confidence-teens

Nemours KidsHealth. (2023). Feeling Good About Yourself (Self-Esteem) (for Kids). https://kidshealth.org/en/kids/self-esteem.html

Roshni, H. (2023). Embrace your uniqueness. Medium. from https://medium.com/@humairaroshni111/embrace-your-uniqueness-26ff9c428615

## Chapter 8

How to Seek Out and Celebrate Diversity In and Out of Your Community. (2019, February 19th). https://www.brighthorizons.com/resources/Article/ideas-embrace-diversity-in-community

Yahoo News. (2020, June 9th). Building teens' respect for diversity: Here's what to know. https://www.yahoo.com/lifestyle/building-teens-respect-diversity-heres-132000368.html

Today.com. (2020, June 10th). Teaching teens to respect diversity: Here's what to know. https://www.today.com/parenting-guides/teaching-teens-respect-diversity-t179025

## Chapter 9

Today.com. (2020, February 1st). Supporting teens' curiosity: Here's what to know. https://www.today.com/parenting-guides/supporting-teens-curiosity-t179077

Center for Parent and Teen Communication. (2021, August 24). Five Ways to Fuel Teen Curiosity. https://parentandteen.com/five-ways-to-fuel-teen-curiosity/

Connections Academy. (2021, October 13). 5 Strategies to Inspire Curiosity in Students. https://www.connectionsacademy.com/support/resources/article/5-strategies-to-inspire-curiosity-in-students/

Greater Good Science Center at the University of California, Berkeley. (2023). Four ways to inspire humble curiosity in your students. https://greatergood.berkeley.edu/article/item/four_ways_to_inspire_humble_curiosity_in_your_students

## | Chapter 10

Positive Psychology. (2019, February 19th). Teaching emotional intelligence. Retrieved from https://positivepsychology.com/teaching-emotional-intelligence/

American Psychological Association. (2019, December 12th). Students do better in school when they can understand, manage emotions. https://www.apa.org/news/press/releases/2019/12/students-manage-emotions

KidsHealth. (2021, January 29th). Emotional Intelligence (for Teens). https://kidshealth.org/en/teens/eq.html

Parent Cue. (2022, March 10th). How to Foster Emotional Intelligence in Kids & Teens. https://theparentcue.org/raising-emotionally-intelligent-teens/